D1275452

TOTALLY Tubular QUILTS

A New Strip-Piecing Technique

RITA HUTCHENS

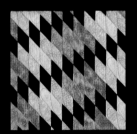
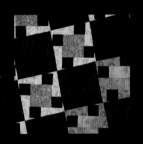
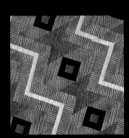
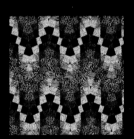

C&T PUBLISHING

©2003, Rita Hutchens

Editor-in-Chief: Darra Williamson

Editor: Pamela Mostek

Technical Editors: Pamela Mostek, Joyce Engles Lytle

Copyeditor: Darra Williamson

Proofreader: Stacy Chamness

Cover Designer: Christina D. Jarumay

Design Director/Book Designer: Christina D. Jarumay

Illustrator: Tim Manibusan

Production Assistant: Jeff Carrillo

Photography: Sharon Risedorph

Digital Photography: Diane Pederson

Published by C&T Publishing, Inc., P.O. Box 1456, Lafayette, California 94549

Front cover: *Rainbow 2*

Back cover: *Irish Chain Goes on Safari*

All rights reserved. No part of this work covered by the copyright hereon may be reproduced and used in any form or any means—graphic, electronic, or mechanical, including photocopying, recording, taping, or information storage and retrieval systems—without written permission of the publisher. The copyrights on individual artworks are retained by the artists as noted in *Totally Tubular Quilts*.

Attention Teachers: C&T Publishing, Inc. encourages you to use this book as a text for teaching. Contact us at 800-284-1114 or **www.ctpub.com** for more information about the C&T Teachers Program.

We take great care to ensure that the information included in this book is accurate and presented in good faith, but no warranty is provided nor results guaranteed. Since we have no control over the choices of materials or procedures used, neither the author nor C&T Publishing, Inc. shall have any liability to any person or entity with respect to any loss or damage caused directly or indirectly by the information contained in this book. For your convenience, we post an up-to-date listing of corrections on our web page (**www.ctpub.com**). If a correction is not already noted, please contact our customer service department at **ctinfo@ctpub.com** or at P.O. Box 1456, Lafayette, California 94549.

Trademarked (™) and Registered Trademark (®) names are used throughout this book. Rather than use the symbols with every occurrence of a trademark and registered trademark name, we are using the names only in the editorial fashion and to the benefit of the owner, with no intention of infringement.

Library of Congress Cataloging-in-Publication Data

Hutchens, Rita.

   Totally tubular quilts : a new strip-piecing technique / Rita Hutchens.
       p. cm.
   Includes bibliographical references and index.
   ISBN 1-57120-208-0
   1. Strip quilting–Patterns. 2. Patchwork–Patterns. I. Title.
   TT835.H88 2003
   746.46'041–dc21
                                                    2003001295

Printed in China

10 9 8 7 6 5 4 3 2 1

Dedication

This book is dedicated to my grandmother, Alice, who taught me to sew;
to my mother, Nancy, and my Aunt Rita who taught me to live from my heart;
and for my daughter, Aleya, so that she can learn to live from hers.

Acknowledgments

I would like to thank my family and friends, for believing in me, and for mostly thinking I was not crazy.

I would also like to thank the community of Sandpoint for supporting me as much as you have over the years, the teachers I have had in life and in quilting, and everyone who has encouraged me to write this book.

Here are some people to whom I would like to give a very special thank-you:

My daughter Aleya for putting up with all of those late dinners and for all of your honest comments like, "That's bad, Mom." I trust your innocent, unbiased intuition when it comes to my work.

Chris White for supporting and encouraging my passions and for being there for the journey.

Marty Bowne for all of the incredible input, ideas, encouragement, information, and suggestions you have given me.

Risa Devore for all of your invaluable energy and support and for helping me choose fabrics and projects for this book.

Mary Bowne for becoming my instant friend and taking me to Quilting by the Sound.

Ken Rose for sharing Nancy's studio with me, which is where it all began.

QZ Allard and Sydnie Stern for helping out in a pinch.

Michael and Rebecca Abolafia, Dianne Croal, Linda Knower, Steve and Cherie Murphy, Gordy and Kathy Robinson, and Chris White for loaning back your quilts to use in this book.

Quilt artists Mary Lou Weidman, Paula Nadelstern, Lorraine Torrance, David Walker, and Genie Barnes for their time.

Quilters Dawn Kelly, Regina Mills, and Roberta Rose-Kanauth for quilting my quilts.

Randy Schaffer at Omnigrid for sending a box of rulers all of those years ago. It changed the way I worked.

Thanks to Husqvarna Viking for sending the wonderful Quilt Designer sewing machine, Timeless Treasures for the beautiful fabrics for the Pinwheels and Lightning projects, Quilters Dream Batting for providing Dream Cotton batting for the projects, Rowenta for the Steam Generator Iron, Ott-Lite for the Vision Saver Portable Magnifier Lamp, and Granny Thimbles Quilt Cottage and Pacific Crescent Quilting for providing fabric.

TABLE OF

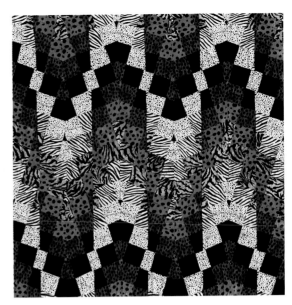

CONTENTS

A Little Background

I remember dresses with pinafores and ruffled aprons my grandmother made for me using an old treadle sewing machine in the family basement. I learned to knit and sew by the age of eight and grew up where a door-to-door fabric man would come to our house with books of fabric. My grandmother and I would choose the pieces we liked best. Then I would have the pleasure of watching her transform them into something beautiful, which was often something for me to wear. That was a special time reserved for my grandmother and me, a sweet memory. Thus, my love of fabric and sewing began.

Combining my love of sewing with the influence of the late 60s and early 70s, I made lots of funky clothing for myself. The high school I attended had a well-developed art program where my love of the arts began to flourish. Growing up outside of New York City, I would go to offbeat gallery shows and major art and craft museums where I was exposed to a whole world of art and creativity. At school one could find me mostly in the craft room, dabbling in jewelry, pottery, and weaving.

At home I always had some kind of sewing, beading, weaving, or basket-making project going amidst the confusion of my extended family, and I was the most happy when creating.

To pursue my passion for art, I went to the State University of New York at New Paltz, where I had the opportunity to study the principles of design and color. With my offbeat sense of design and unconventional sense of color, the desire to create in a unique, individual way began to germinate.

In 1980 I began strip piecing and made my first quilt using the Seminole technique, intuitively using the principles of design and color learned in college. Fascinated by the infinite combinations of color and pattern, I became instantly aware of the graphic and visual possibilities of pieced fabric.

While exploring the technique of Seminole strip piecing, I began to notice that the triangles cut off at the top of the pieced strip could fill in the triangles cut off at the bottom. If the two were somehow connected, no triangles would have to be cut off, and there would be no waste. I discovered the best way to do this was to sew the strip sets that the pieces were cut from into tubes, so I began making very small tubes for my Seminole patterns.

Ironing the seams on these small pieces was tedious, and cutting the tubes apart was confusing. I discovered that if I made enough repetitions of the strips, they would fit around the ironing board, making piecing, ironing the seams, and cutting the tubes apart much easier and faster. I developed a way to draft patterns for this type of piecing, made yards and yards of pattern strips, and put them as borders and trim on just about anything I could sew them to. I began combining these pattern strips with other strips to create more intricate patterns, began to think of my patterns as "fabric," and went on to making yards and yards of this fabric. For eight years I had a

business making and selling one-of-a-kind and limited-edition wearable art made out of my pieced fabric.

I had little exposure to contemporary or traditional quiltmaking, so I had no preconceived ideas of how to make quilts. Through lots of experimentation and mistakes, I developed a style and process of working that was all my own. Seminole piecing techniques, Amish quilts, and some pictures in a calendar book of Nancy Crow's quilts were the biggest influences. Sometimes it is a great advantage not to know the "right" way to do something. When we don't know the "rules," we are forced to be innovative and come up with our own unique ideas and ways of doing things.

This book is a result of 23 years of experimenting and perfecting this unique technique, which I am pleased to have the opportunity to share with you. I have presented an array of projects that you can create as you are learning about this process. Once you understand the concept, I encourage you to try your own designs.

For every quilt I have made and loved, there has been one that I have not, but I have learned from every one of those quilts I disliked. What I thought was a problem often lead to a completely new concept. I encourage you to think of mistakes as intuitive decisions: use and almost welcome them. Trust what you are given. Some of my best quilts have been made from fabrics that have landed next to each other in the pile that tends to accumulate on my floor, or made from a piece of almost hopeless fabric that jumped out at me screaming for help. Most of all, take the risk, go for the challenge, and enjoy the process. Do not fret about the outcome or the fabrics used. The unknown results are part of the fun!

—Rita

The Totally Tubular Technique

The possibilities are endless with this new and innovative method of strip piecing. You can create hearts, diamonds, squares, triangles, spirals, and other geometric designs. Mirror-image patterns become easy, opening a whole range of possibilities for making kaleidoscopes and symmetrical designs. There are no templates used in this technique. A see-through ruler, scissors, and rotary cutter are all you need to make these intricate and distinctive patterns. Just follow the step-by-step instructions, and the results will be spectacular.

You begin by sewing together strips to make a piece of striped fabric. This striped fabric is then sewn into a tube, and then cut into strips again. These strips are rearranged to make a quilt pattern. This pattern is sewn into another tube and then cut into more strips, rearranged, and sewn back together into another pattern. These steps are repeated as many times as necessary to obtain the desired result.

The more you cut the pattern apart, the more intricate the design becomes. Tiny pieces appear that you would not have attempted to cut with templates. It is just a matter of following the steps to create a quilt that is truly outstanding. Before you start, a few tips about fabric and tools will help make your Totally Tubular experience one you will want to repeat again and again.

Getting Started

Fabric

Choosing the fabric, for some of us, can be a scary thing. What if I choose the "wrong" fabric? What if no one else likes what I choose? Maybe you've had these thoughts yourself as you stand in the quilt shop surrounded by thousands of gorgeous choices. My best advice when picking out fabric is simple . . . . just relax!

Start with two or three inspiring fabrics, ones that immediately catch your eye as you study the selection. Fill in your two or three inspiring fabrics with others that complement them—that have colors and values that graduate and transition into each other. Include a wide range of values from light to dark. More contrast in your fabrics will create more drama in your final quilt.

You may want to choose a theme for your fabrics. Examples of themes could be fabrics with lines, squares, stripes, or other geomtrics; pastel fabrics; primary or secondary colors; fabrics with animal prints; or hand-dyed batiks. You can make up any theme you want. Picking a theme helps to narrow down your selection from the seemingly unlimited choices and alleviates a little confusion and "buyer anxiety!"

If you're stuck, hold up your fabrics to a mirror, or take a photo with a Polaroid or digital camera in both color and in black and white. Viewing your selections in black and white helps you to see value and gradations. If you're computer savvy, try scanning in the fabrics and taking a look at all of them on the screen at once. In other words, change your perspective a little.

Once you've made your selections, I recommend washing and drying your fabric, and then folding it in half selvage to selvage and ironing it before you begin sewing.

Tools

Choosing the right tools for the job and using them in a consistent manner makes all tasks easier and quicker, and ensures accuracy. Here are the tools I think are "must haves" and some optional tools I like to have on hand—

■ 6" x 24" see-through Omnigrid ruler with $^1/_8$" and $^1/_4$" markings and a 45°line

■ 3" x 18" Omnigrid ruler with markings for ease of use

■ Large cutting mat (at least 24" in one direction, preferably 30" x 36")

■ 45mm or larger rotary cutter with a sharp blade

■ Sharp scissors

■ Pins. I use quilters' pins with white heads, mostly so my family can find them on the floor.

■ Marking pencils with sharp points for light and dark fabrics

■ Pencil sharpener to keep pencils sharp for marking dots and lines accurately

■ Spray bottle (optional)

■ A hot steam iron. I like to use a Rowenta Steam Generator Iron.

■ A 4' metal ruler (optional) is handy for marking long cutting lines or squaring off your quilt.

■ Most importantly, your sense of adventure and willingness to explore and try new things.

A Look at the Steps

Now that you have your fabric selected and your tools assembled, you are ready to take a look at this exciting new technique. In the following pages, you'll find a step-by-step explanation of the process with accompanying how-to photos. Each of the projects in the book follows this basic order, yet you will find variations in each of them. You may want to refer back to this section as you work on your quilt.

Cutting the Strips

Strips are the foundation of the pattern, so it is very important to cut them accurately. Cut your strips the full width of the fabric, which is approximately 42". Use a sharp rotary cutter and 6" x 24" see-through ruler.

Fold the fabric in half selvage to selvage, and turn it so the fold is closest to you. Place the short end of the ruler along the fold of the fabric and the long side along the raw edge of the fabric. Trim the raw edge to straighten and square as shown, and then cut the required strips.

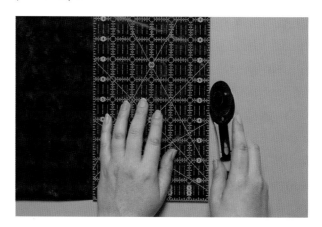

TIP *To make sure your ruler doesn't slip while you are cutting, attach sticky sandpaper dots to the underside of the ruler. Look for these dots at your favorite quilt or fabric store. You can also purchase rulers with sandpaper-type dots already attached to prevent slipping.*

Two of the projects, *Rainbow* on page 24 and *Lightning* on page 40, are diamond patterns and begin with strips that have a right triangle cut off one end. If you are making one of these quilts, cut the required strips, and then cut a small right triangle off the end of each strip using the 45° marking on your ruler as a guide.

Sewing the Strips Together

Before you begin sewing, adjust the stitch length on your sewing machine so that you are making a stitch that is slightly shorter than your usual sewing stitch, or approximately 22 stitches per inch. Make sure that your $1/4$" seam gauge is accurate as you will be making $1/4$" seams for each project unless noted differently in the project directions. Sewing your strips together with a careful, accurate seam allowance helps ensure that you will be pleased with your finished quilt.

Without pinning, stretching, or pulling, gently feed the strips through your sewing machine, matching the edges and keeping an even $1/4$" seam allowance. Begin by sewing the strips together in pairs. Then sew the pairs together to make groups of four, and sew the groups of four strips together. Continue working this way until all of your strips are sewn together to make the desired strip set. Don't worry about keeping the ends even at this point. You will do that when you trim the strip sets.

When you are sewing strips together that have a right triangle cut off, begin sewing the seam from the cut off end of the strip, matching up the beginning of the seam as shown. All of the projects will have "steps" where diamonds are sewn together. Follow this method whenever you sew any two diamonds together.

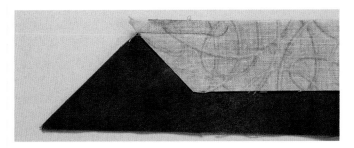

Don't be overwhelmed by the number of strips you are sewing together. Remember, you're sewing together strips for the whole quilt at once. Take time to carefully press your seams open as you sew, using a hot steam iron to ensure that your strip set is flat and easy to work with.

Squaring, Trimming, and Cutting
SQUARE PATTERNS

After your strip set is sewn together and pressed, the next step is to trim and square up the ends. Turn the strip set so the seams run horizontally. Place the 6" end of your 6" x 24" ruler even with the bottom edge of the strip set. With the seams of the strip set square to the 6" lines of the ruler, use your rotary cutter to trim off a scant edge along the 24" side of the ruler as shown.

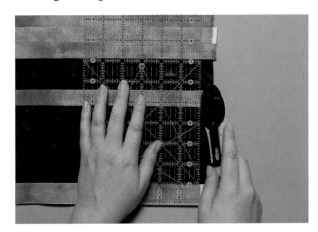

The next step is to cut the strip set in half across the width so that you have two strips sets that are each 21" wide. An easy way to do this is to fold the set in half and iron the fold. Unfold the strip set and cut on the folded line, making sure that everything is square.

Then turn the 21" strip sets so the seams run vertically, place them side by side, and sew them together to make strip bands as shown for each project. Enough strips are sewn together so when the completed strip band is sewn into a tube, it will fit around the ironing board.

DIAMOND PATTERNS

If you are working with a diamond pattern, do not cut the strip sets in half. After you have sewn your diamond strip sets together into a strip band, you will need to trim both ends at a 45° angle. Position the 45° marking on your ruler on the long edge of the strip band. Check the seams of the strips to make sure they are lined up with this same 45° angle. (The 24" edge of your ruler is on the bias edge of the strip band.) Trim off a scant edge with your rotary cutter.

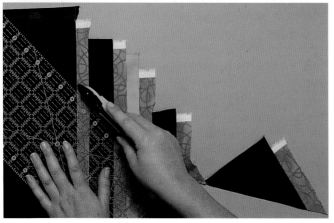

Making a Tube

The next seam you sew transforms your strip band into the first tube.

SQUARE TUBES

Beginning the seam from the edge you just trimmed off, sew the top strip of the strip band to the bottom strip of the same strip band, making it into a tube. Turn the tube inside out, place it around the ironing board, and press the seam open as shown. Turn the tube right side out and press again.

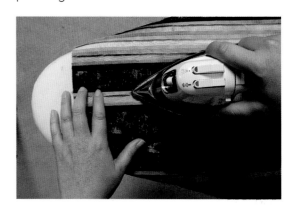

DIAMOND TUBES

Note: The instructions for each Totally Tubular project include other tubes besides the basic square and diamond tubes. Use the following directions for making these tubes, each of which begins as a flat, diamond shape.

The seams of a diamond tube spiral around the tube, so you will need to ease in enough "flatness" to pin and sew the top and bottom strip of the strip band into a tube. After you have pinned and stitched the seam, turn the tube inside out. Press the seam open, rotating the tube around the ironing board. Turn the tube right side out and press again.

Cutting Continuous Strips

Continuous strips are cut from a tube. They have no beginning and no end. They are rotated and sewn back together to create the pattern. Generally, one continuous strip has all of the elements in it to make one complete repeat of the pattern.

SQUARE PATTERNS

Square up the tube by placing the 6" edge of your ruler along one fold line of the tube. Trim off a scant edge along the long side of the ruler. Fold the tube completely flat. Working from this trimmed edge, accurately measure the required strip width and use your rotary cutter to cut through both layers of the folded tube. Continue cutting strips this way, checking that the fold, seams, ruler, and edges of the tube all remain square.

DIAMOND PATTERNS

If you are cutting continuous strips for a diamond pattern, the tube will look different than the tube for a square pattern. The seams will be at a 45° angle to the fold of the fabric and edge of the tube. Fold the tube completely flat. Place the short edge of the ruler along one fold and the long edge along the raw edge of the fabric. Check your seams to make sure they match the 45° line on the ruler. Working from this trimmed edge, accurately measure the required strip width, and use your rotary cutter to cut through both layers of the folded tube.

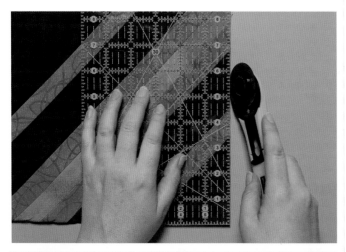

Sewing Continuous Strips Together

In this step, you rotate the strips around to make the pattern and then sew them together to form a pattern tube. Use pins to match up the seams. Sewing two continuous strips together establishes the pattern, so make sure you are consistent when rotating the strips. Each project has specific instructions to match up the continuous strips for that project. Begin by sewing them together in pairs. Then sew the pairs together to make groups of four, and sew the groups of four together to make the pattern tube. Press the seams open as you sew, rotating the continuous strips around the ironing board. Turn the tube right side out and press again.

TIP *If your sewing machine has a free arm with an attachable sewing table, you might be tempted to remove the table since you are sewing a continuous seam. Instead, leave the sewing table in position on the machine when sewing together continuous strips; this will make it easier for you to keep the pressed seams open.*

Marking and Cutting the Pattern Tube

Now that you have carefully sewn your pattern tube together, it's time to cut it apart again! With the *Totally Tubular* technique, the more you cut apart the pieces you have sewn together, the more intricate your pattern becomes.

Each project shows you where to mark dots and connect them with a cutting line. Mark any dots along the raw edge inward $1/4$" to allow for the $1/4$" seam allowance. Draw the cutting line from one raw edge of the tube to the other. You may have to rotate the tube around to complete the line.

Use scissors to cut along the drawn line through one layer of the tube. Your fabric will be flat again and ready for the next step.

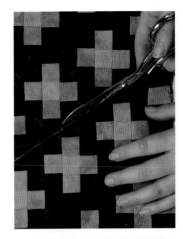

Repeating the Steps

Now that you are familiar with the basic steps, you are ready to create the designs in this book. These basic steps are used to create each quilt, but they are repeated with slight variations to complete a variety of dramatic designs. The step-by-step instructions for each project explain and show you how to cut, rearrange, and resew to create the quilt.

Each project focuses on a slightly different concept, increasing your skills as the book progresses. Besides following the steps to create each of the quilts, elements of some of them can be used for borders or blocks in other quilts as well.

Once you've tried some of the projects in this book, you may want to try some of your own designs. For the adventurous, I encourage experimentation, playfulness, and going out on a limb to try something new.

Jacks

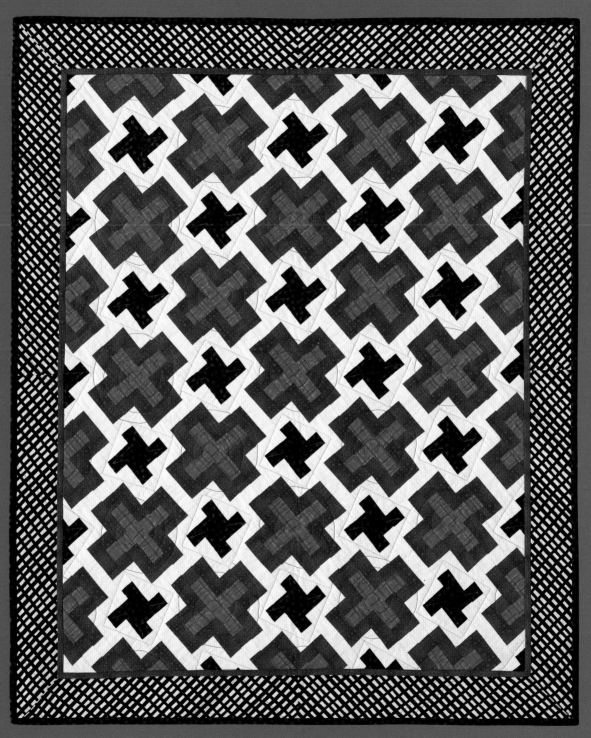

Designed and made by Rita Hutchens and quilted by Risa Devore, 2002. Finished size: 33" x 40"

This simple repeat pattern draws the eye in and adds a great deal of movement. Shapes appear to be twirling around, transforming what could be a very ordinary pattern into something very lively. I designed this quilt after doing some of my own batiks. I wanted a quilt with shapes surrounded by a white line much like a wax-resist line in batiks.

Fabric Requirements and Cutting List

All yardages given are based on 42"-wide fabric, and strips are cut the full width of the fabric. Refer to Cutting the Strips on page 12.

FABRIC	AMOUNT	CUTTING
■ Blue	$7/8$ yard	Six $1^1/4$" strips
		Six $2^3/4$" strips
■ Pink	$3/8$ yard	Four $1^1/4$" strips
		One $4^1/4$" strip
■ Black	$1/3$ yard	Two $2^3/4$" strips
		Two $1^1/4$" strips
□ White	$7/8$ yard	Six $1^1/4$" strips
		Four $2^3/4$" strips
		One 5" strip
Narrow border	$1/4$ yard	Four 1" strips
Wide border	$1/2$ yard	Four $3^1/4$" strips
Backing	$1^1/3$ yards	
Batting	39" x 46" piece	
Binding	$3/8$ yard	Four $2^3/4$" strips

Directions

1. Referring to Sewing the Strips Together on page 13, sew the strips together as shown into 8 strip sets. Make two of strip set 1, one of strip set 2, two of strip set 3, two of strip set 4, and one of strip set 5. Press the seams open as you sew.

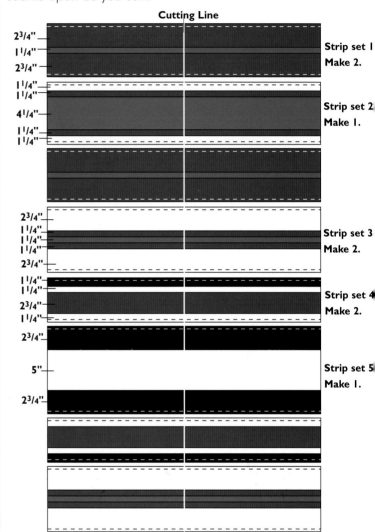

2. Referring to Squaring, Trimming, and Cutting on page 13, square and trim the ends of the strip sets. Using a rotary cutter and ruler, cut each strip set in half on the cutting line shown in Step 1. You will now have 16 strip sets, each approximately 21" in width.

3. Sew the strip sets from Step 2 together as shown to make a strip band. Press the seams open as you sew. Make 2 strip bands. Note the fold lines as shown.

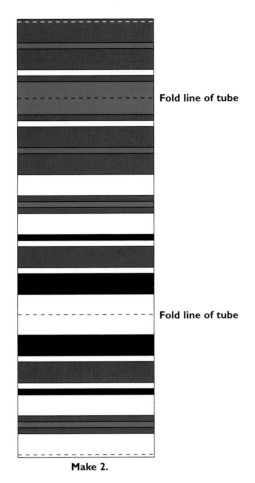

Fold line of tube

Fold line of tube

Make 2.

4. Sew the top of the strip band from Step 3 to the bottom of the same strip band, making a tube. Repeat to make 2 tubes. Press the seams open, placing the tube around the ironing board. Fold the tube on the fold lines as shown. Check to see that the seams are parallel to the fold. Referring to Cutting Continuous Strips on page 15, use a rotary cutter and ruler to cut through both layers of the tube to cut twenty-seven 1¹/₄" continuous strips.

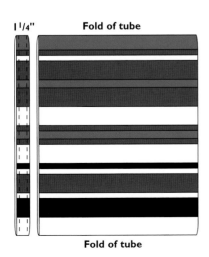

1¹/₄" **Fold of tube**

Fold of tube

5. Line up the pairs of the continuous strips cut in Step 4 as shown. There will be one extra strip.

Fold of tube Fold of tube

6. Rotate the top continuous strip from Step 5 to the right to make the pattern as shown. Pin together matching seams and sew. Press the seams open, rotating the continuous strips around the ironing board. Make 13 pairs.

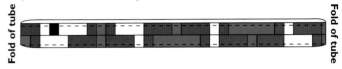

Fold of tube Fold of tube

7. To make the pattern tube, pin and sew the 13 pairs of continuous strips from Step 6 together as shown. When you are matching up the pattern, always rotate the top group of continuous strips to the right. Sew the remaining strip to either end of the tube. Press the seams open as you sew. Referring to Marking and Cutting the Pattern Tube on page 17, mark the dots as shown, making sure that you mark the dots along the raw edge on the ¹/₄" seam allowance. Using your ruler, connect the dots with a drawn line.

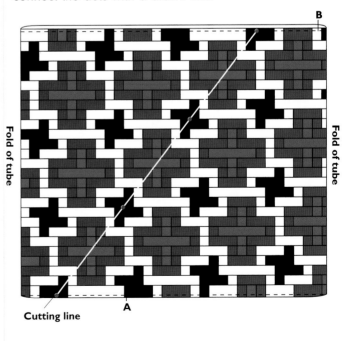

B

Fold of tube Fold of tube

Cutting line A

8. Using scissors, cut along the drawn line through one layer of the pattern tube to make it into a flat diamond shape. Sew together the long sides of the diamond shape to form another tube. Bring the seam at Point A up to match the seam at Point B and pin. Pin the other matching seams along this edge and sew, easing in flatness; the seam will spiral around the tube. Press the seam open. The flat diamond shape becomes a tube again.

A —

Cutting line

B —

Cutting line

9. Mark a cutting line on the tube sewn in Step 8, square to the cut ends and parallel to the fold of the tube as shown. Using scissors, cut on the drawn line through one layer of the tube to make a flat rectangle.

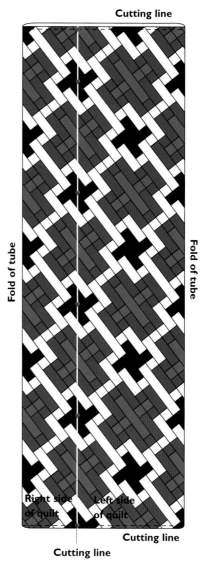

Cutting line

Fold of tube

Fold of tube

Right side of quilt

Left side of quilt

Cutting line

Cutting line

10. To make the pattern of the quilt the same at the top and bottom, mark and cut along the drawn line as shown.

> **TIP** *Use the section that you trimmed in step 11 as the start of a pillow to match your quilt, or cut it up into blocks and use it for another quilt, as in the Pinwheels variation on page 39.*

11. Sew the 4 narrow border strips to the 4 wide border strips. Referring to Borders on page 76, add mitered borders to the quilt in your preferred method.

12. Refer to page 76 for tips and information to help you complete your quilt.

Cutting line

Cutting line

Cutting line

Left side of quilt

Right side of quilt

Rainbow

Designed and made by Rita Hutchens and quilted by Dawn Kelly, 2002. Finished size: 38" x 46"

Rainbow quilts are so pleasing to the eye. You can never go wrong making one. Some quilters are skeptical of piecing with fabric that is cut off the grain; however, I had never been told how touchy it can be to work with, so I never had a problem with it.

Fabric Requirements and Cutting List

All yardages given are based on 42"-wide fabric, and strips are cut the full width of the fabric. Refer to Cutting the Strips on page 12.

FABRIC	AMOUNT	CUTTING
Red, orange, yellow	⅓ yard of each color	Four 2" strips of each color
Green, blue, purple	⅝ yard of each color.	Four 2" strips of each color Six 1¼" strips of each color
Black	1⅔ yards	Twelve 2" strips Six 1¼" strips Six 4" strips
Backing	1½ yards	
Batting	44" x 52" piece	
Binding	½ yard	Five 2¾" strips

Directions

1. Referring to Cutting the Strips on page 12, cut a small right triangle off the end of each strip as shown to make a diamond pattern. Make sure that each triangle is cut in the same direction.

2. Referring to Sewing Strips Together on page 13, sew the strips together as shown for a diamond pattern. Using a black strip as the middle strip of each strip set, sew together 2 strip sets for each of the 6 colors, totaling 12 strip sets. Press the seams open as you sew.

Make 2 for each color.

3. Sew the strip sets from Step 2 together as shown to make a strip band. Press the seams open as you sew. Make 2 strip bands. Referring to Squaring, Trimming, and Cutting on page 13, square and trim the ends of the diamond strip band.

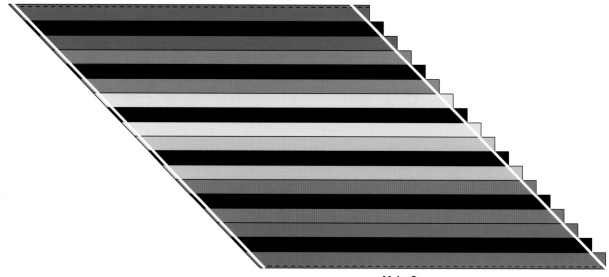

Make 2.

4. Referring to Making a Tube on page 14, sew the top of the strip band from Step 3 to the bottom of the same strip band, making a tube. Repeat to make two identical tubes. Press the seams open, rotating the tube around the ironing board, and fold the tube as shown. Referring to Cutting Continuous Strips for Diamond Patterns on page 16, use a rotary cutter and ruler to cut through both layers of the tube to cut ten 2" continuous strips from each tube.

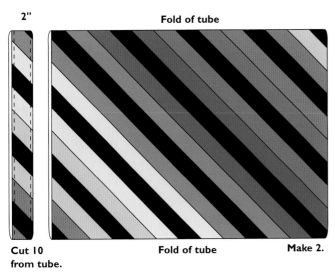

2"   **Fold of tube**

Cut 10 from tube.   **Fold of tube**   **Make 2.**

5. To help match the pattern accurately for pinning, mark a dot on the $^1/_4$" seamline of every black diamond as shown. Line up the pairs of continuous strips as shown.

Fold of tube

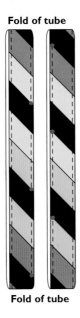

Fold of tube

6. Rotate the right hand strip down, matching the dots as shown to form the pattern. Pin together, matching dots, and sew. Press the seams open, rotating the continuous strips around the ironing board. Make 10 pairs.

Fold of tube

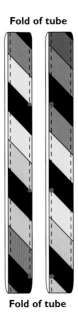

Fold of tube

7. Sew 2 pairs of continuous strips from Step 6 together as shown. Always rotate the right-hand group of continuous strips down to match the pattern. Press the seams open as you sew. Make 5.

Fold of tube

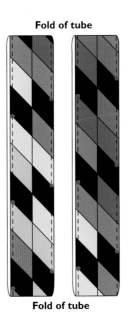

Fold of tube

8. To complete the pattern tube, pin and sew the units from Step 7 together as shown. Continue matching dots, pinning, sewing, and pressing as you did in Steps 6 and 7. Referring to Marking and Cutting the Pattern Tube on page 17, mark a cutting line square to the raw edge and parallel to the fold of the tube as shown.

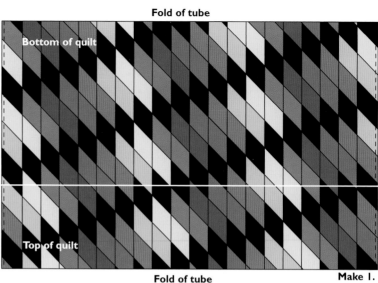

Fold of tube

Bottom of quilt

Cutting line

Top of quilt

Fold of tube   Make 1.

9. Using scissors, cut along the drawn line through one layer of the pattern tube to make it into a flat rectangle shape. Your quilt is now ready for a border.

10. Make strip sets for the border as shown in the color photo on page 25. Piece together 2 strips of each border fabric to make each side border. Referring to Borders on page 76, add mitered your borders to the quilt in preferred method.

11. Refer to page 76 for tips and information to help you complete your quilt.

Cutting line

Top of quilt

Bottom of quilt

Cutting line

Another Version - *Rainbow 2*. Designed and made by
Rita Hutchens and quilted by Regina Mills, 2002.
Finished size: 40" x 44".
I've used the same continuous strips as in *Rainbow*
except I've rotated and matched them up in a
different way.

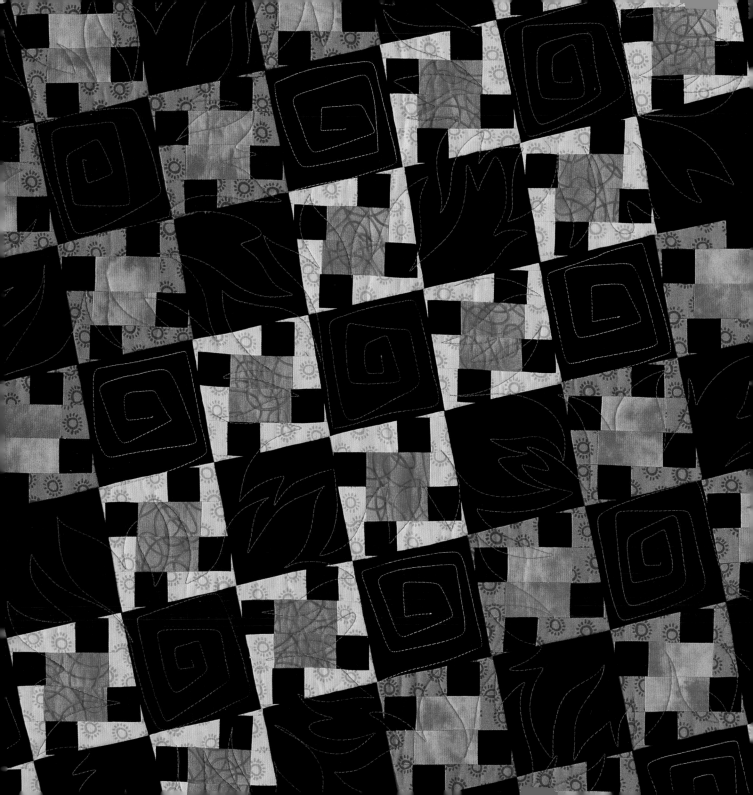

Pinwheels

Designed and made by Rita Hutchens and quilted by Dawn Kelly, 2002. Finished size 29" x 38"

I have made this design many times and am always happily surprised at the transformation of positive and negative space as the pattern develops. I took advantage of the seam allowances to create the little hooks on the ends of the pinwheels, a discovery made quite by accident.

Fabric Requirements and Cutting List

All yardages given are based on 42"-wide fabric, and strips are cut the full width of the fabric. Refer to Cutting the Strips on page 12.

FABRIC	AMOUNT	CUTTING
■ Black	1½ yards	Eight 1½" strips Eight strips to be cut and added later
■■ Turquoise, pink	⅓ yard of each color	Two 2½" strips of each color
■■ Green, blue	½ yard of each color	One 5½" strip of each color One 2½" strip of each color Two 1½" strips of each color
Back	1⅓" yards	
Batting	35" x 44" piece	
Binding	½ yard	Four 3½" strips

Directions

1. Referring to Sewing the Strips Together on page 13, sew the strips together as shown into 4 strip sets. Make 2 strip sets for the pink and turquoise color scheme and 2 strip sets for the green and blue color scheme. Press the seams open as you sew.

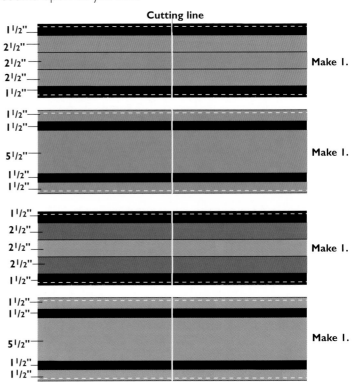

2. Referring to Squaring, Trimming, and Cutting on page 13, square and trim the ends of the strip sets. Using a rotary cutter and ruler, cut each strip set in half on the cutting line shown in Step 1. You will now have 4 strip sets for each color scheme, each approximately 21" in width.

3. Sew the strip sets together as shown to make 1 strip band for each color scheme. Press the seams open as you sew. Note the fold line as shown.

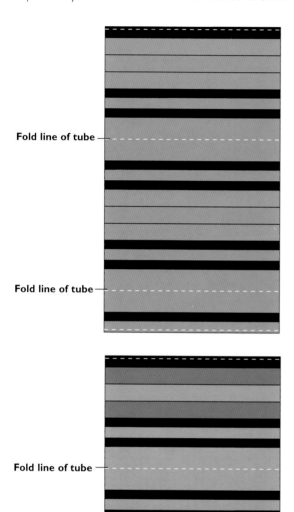

Make 1 for each color scheme.

4. Sew the top strip of the unit from Step 3 to the bottom strip of the same unit, making a tube. Make 1 tube for each color scheme. Press the seams open, placing the tube around the ironing board. Fold the tube on the fold lines as shown. Check to see that the seams are parallel to the fold of the tube. Referring to Cutting Continuous Strips on page 15, use a rotary cutter and ruler to cut through both layers of the tube, and cut ten 1¹/₂"-wide continuous strips from each tube.

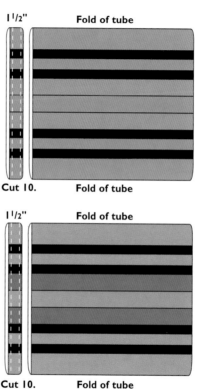

5. Line up pairs of continuous strips from Step 4 as shown. Repeat for each color scheme.

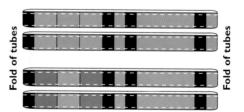

6. Rotate the top continuous strip from Step 5 to the right to make the pattern as shown. Pin together matching seams and sew. Press the seams open, rotating the continuous strips around the ironing board. Make 5 pairs for each color scheme.

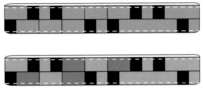

Make 5 for each color scheme.

7. To make the pattern tube, pin and sew 5 pairs of continuous strips from Step 6 together as shown. When you are matching up the pattern, always rotate the top group of continuous strips to the right. Press the seams open as you sew. Make one pattern tube for each color scheme. Referring to Marking and Cutting the Pattern Tube on page 17, mark dots as shown. Using your ruler, connect the dots with a drawn line.

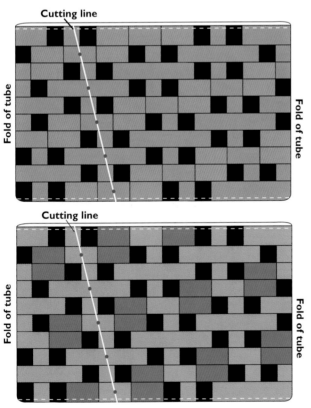

Make 5 for each color scheme.

8. Using scissors, cut along the drawn line through one layer of the tube to make it into a flat diamond shape. Repeat for each tube. Referring to Marking and Cutting the Pattern Tube on page 17, mark dots as shown. Using your ruler, connect the dots with a drawn line to make 3 cutting lines as shown. Repeat for each color scheme.

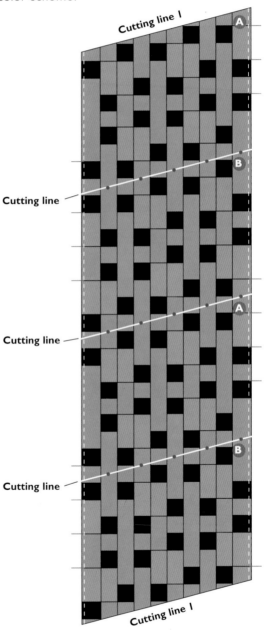

Make 5 for each color scheme.

9. Using a rotary cutter and ruler, cut along the drawn lines to make the diamond shape from Step 8 into 2 matching pairs of sub-units labeled A or B as shown. Pin and sew the A and B sub-units together, matching the seams as shown. Make 2 of these units for each color scheme.

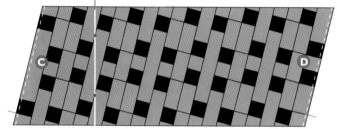

Make 2 for each color scheme.

10. Draw dots as shown and mark cutting line 2. Repeat for all 4 units.

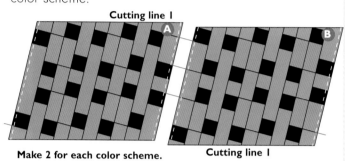

Make 2 for each color scheme.

11. Using a rotary cutter and ruler, cut on cutting line 2, making each unit into 2 sub-units labeled C and D. Rearrange sub-units C and D as shown. Match seams along the marked seamline, and pin and sew into one unit. Make 2 for each color scheme.

Make 2 for each color scheme.

12. Mark cutting line 3 as shown. Using your rotary cutter and ruler, cut along the drawn line to make 2 narrow strips from each unit as shown. Repeat for all 4 units making 4 strips in each color scheme.

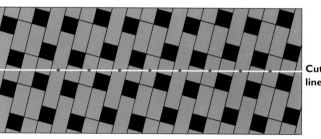

13. Referring to Cutting the Strips on page 12, cut 8 black strips that are the same width and approximately 2" longer than the pattern strips from Step 12.

14. Pin and sew one black strip onto each pattern strip as shown. (Sewing the more stable addition strip onto the pieced pattern strip keeps the layers from shifting as you sew.) Press the seam towards the black strip. Repeat for the 4 strips in each color scheme for a total of 8 strips.

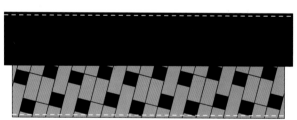

Make 4 for each color scheme.

15. Refer to the diagram below. Sew the units from Step 14 together as shown. Make 2. Press the seams toward the black strips. Mark dots as shown. Using your ruler, connect the dots with 4 drawn lines. Using a rotary cutter and ruler, trim the ends of the black strips even with the end of the pattern strips. Cut on the drawn lines to make 5 strip units as shown. Repeat for each of 2 units to make a total of 10 strip units.

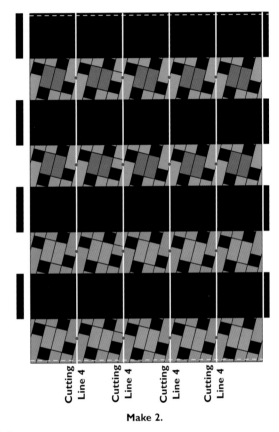

Cutting Line 4 Cutting Line 4 Cutting Line 4 Cutting Line 4

Make 2.

16. Sew one short end of each unit from Step 15 to the other end of the same unit along the marked seamline to make a continuous strip. Repeat for all 10 strip units. Line up pairs of continuous strips as shown.

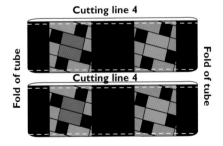

Cutting line 4

Fold of tube

Fold of tube

Cutting line 4

17. Rotate the top continuous strip to the right to form the pattern as shown. Pin together the matching seams and sew using a generous ¼" seam allowance. Press the seams open, rotating the continuous strips around the ironing board. Make 5 pairs.

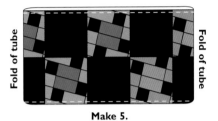

Fold of tube

Fold of tube

Make 5.

18. Using a generous ¼" seam allowance, sew the 5 pairs of continuous strips from Step 16 together as shown to make another pattern tube. Always rotate the top group of continuous strips to the right. Press the seams open as you sew, rotating the strips around the ironing board. When the pattern tube is complete, mark dots along the raw edge inward ¼" as shown to allow for the ¼" seam allowance. Connect the dots with cutting line 5 as shown.

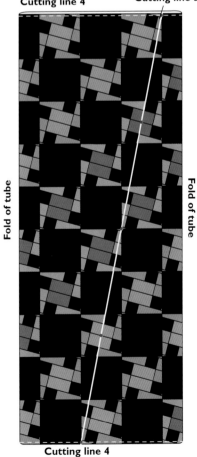

Cutting line 4   Cutting line 5

Fold of tube

Fold of tube

Cutting line 4

Make 1.

19. Using scissors, cut along cutting line 5 through one layer of the tube to make it into a flat diamond shape. Mark dots and connect with cutting line 6 square to cutting line 5 as shown. Using a rotary cutter and ruler, cut on cutting line 6, making each unit into 2 sub-units labeled A and B as shown.

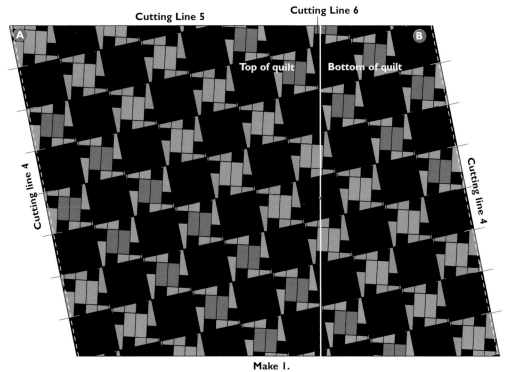

Make 1.

20. Rearrange sub-units A and B as shown. Match the seams along the marked seamline, pin, and sew to make one unit again.

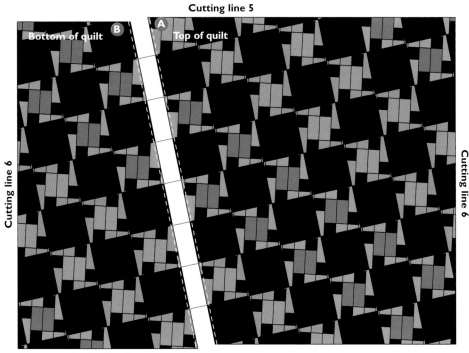

21. Refer to page 76 for tips and information to help
you complete your quilt.

Cutting line 6

Cutting line 6

Another Version - *Spin Wheels*. Designed, quilted, and made by Rita Hutchens, 2002.

Finished size: 21^1/$_2$" x 21^1/$_2$".

I designed and made this quilt by cutting blocks from *Jacks* (page 18), and combining them with blocks cut from *Pinwheels* (page 30).

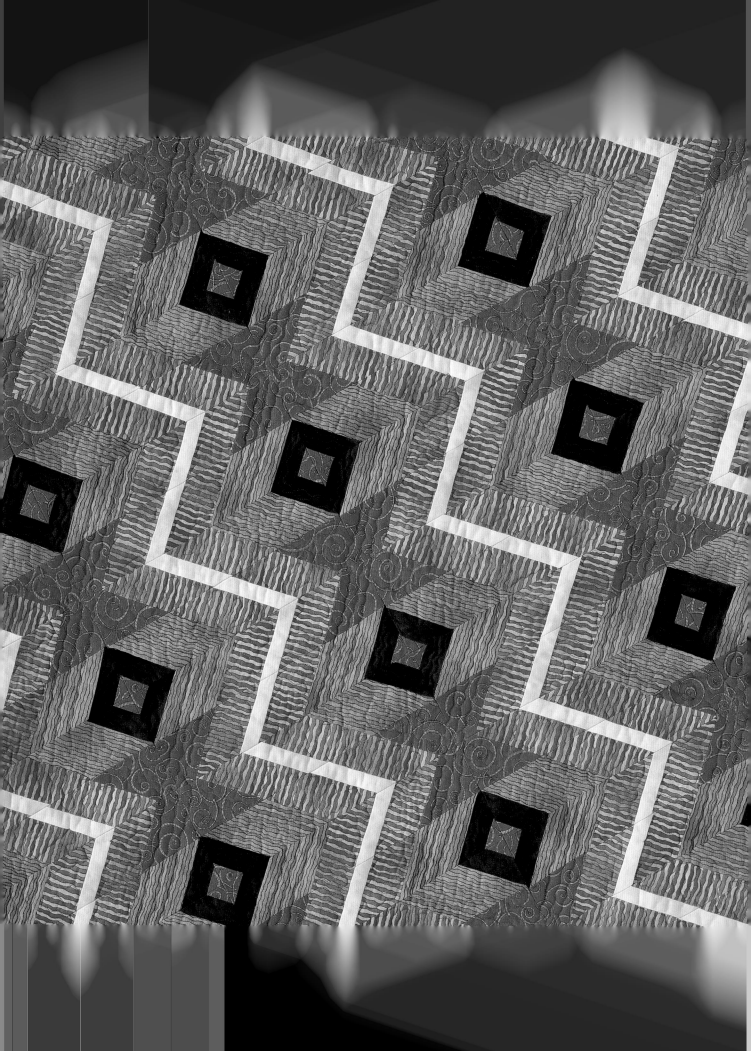

Lightning

Designed and made by Rita Hutchens and quilted by Roberta Rose-Kanauth, 2002. Finished size: 34" x 40"

The secondary colors in this quilt give it a subtle look. Working in mirror image can be fun, especially when you use stripes. With this template-free technique you don't have to fret about which way to position the template so that the stripes run in the desired direction.

Fabric Requirements and Cutting List

All yardages given are based on 42"-wide fabric, and the strips are cut the full width of the fabric. Refer to Cutting the Strips on page 12.

FABRIC	AMOUNT	CUTTING
Peach stripe	$5/8$ yard	Eight $2^1/4$" strips

(Note: Printed stripes must run the width of the fabric.)

FABRIC	AMOUNT	CUTTING
Turquoise stripe	$7/8$ yard	Sixteen $1^3/4$" strips

(Note: Printed stripes must run the length of the fabric.)
If the stripes on your chosen fabric do not run in the required direction, you will need $1^1/4$ yards of fabric, and you will need the strips from this fabric the length of the fabric or parallel to the selvage instead of across the width.

FABRIC	AMOUNT	CUTTING
Purple	$5/8$ yard	Eight $2^1/4$" strips
Brown	$3/8$ yard	Eight $1^1/4$" strips
Light Turquise	$1/3$ yard	Eight 1" strips
Backing	$1^1/3$ yards	
Batting	40" x 46" piece	
Binding	$1/2$ yard	Four $3^1/2$" strips

Working in Mirror Image
You can use this technique to make kaleidoscopes and other mirror-image patterns without using templates. Diamond mirror-image patterns, as you'll find in this project, are made from two different sets of strips with the ends cut off the strips of each set in opposite directions. Make one mirror image following the diagrams, and make the other mirror image by repeating each step exactly the opposite way you did in the first mirror image.

Directions

1. Cut a small right triangle off half of the strips in each fabric with the angle going from top left to bottom right as shown. Cut a small right triangle off the remaining strips of each fabric in the opposite direction as shown.

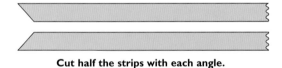

Cut half the strips with each angle.

2. Referring to Sewing the Strips Together on page 13, sew the strip together as shown. Make 4 for each mirror image for a total of 8 strip sets. Press the seams open as you sew.

Make 4 for each mirror image.

3. Continue to work in mirror images, keeping the pieces of each mirror image separate from the pieces of the other. Pin and sew together the 4 strip sets of each mirror image as shown to make a diamond strip band. Press the seams open as you sew. Make one for each mirror image. Press all the seams open as you sew. Referring to Squaring, Trimming, and Cutting on page 13, trim the diamond strip band as shown.

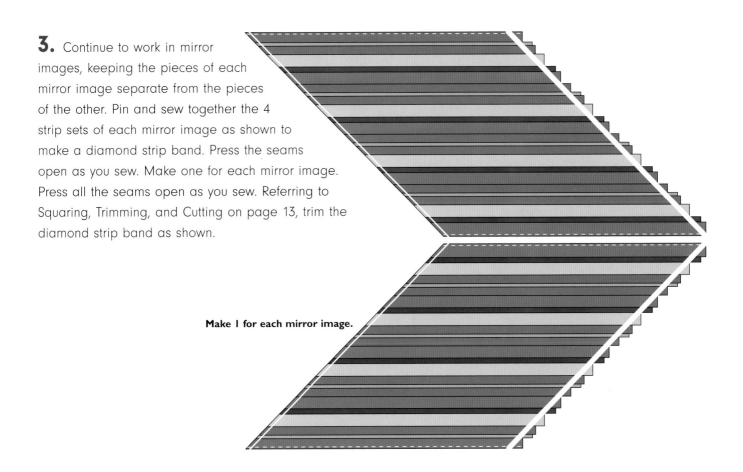

Make 1 for each mirror image.

4. Referring to Making a Tube on page 14, sew the top of the strip band from Step 3 to the bottom of the same strip band, making a tube. Repeat for each mirror image. Press the seams open, rotating the tube around the ironing board, and fold as shown. Referring to Cutting Continuous Strips on page 15, use a rotary cutter and ruler to cut through both layers and cut ten 2$^1/_4$" strips from each pattern tube.

Make 1 for each mirror image.

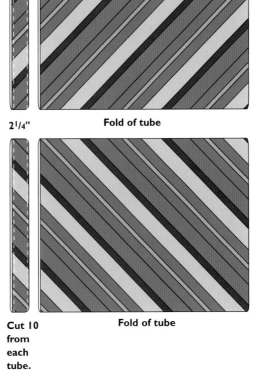

2$^1/_4$" **Fold of tube**

2$^1/_4$" **Fold of tube**

Cut 10 from each tube. **Fold of tube**

5. Mark a dot on the $^1/_4$" seamline in the center of the light turquoise strip as shown. Line up the pairs of continuous strips from Step 4 as shown. Repeat to make 5 for each mirror image, continuing to keep the mirror image pieces separate from each other.

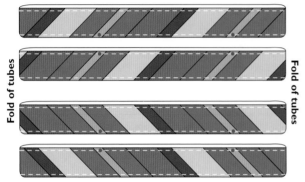

Make 5 for each mirror image.

6. Pin, matching dots, and sew the continuous strips from Step 5 together as shown. Press the seams open, rotating the continuous strips around the ironing board. Repeat, making 5 for each mirror image.

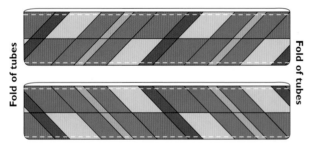

Make 5 for each mirror image.

7. To combine mirror-image pieces, pin and sew together one of each mirror-image unit from Step 6, matching the mirror-image pattern as shown. Press the seams open as you sew. Repeat to make 5.

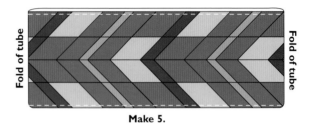

Make 5.

8. To complete the pattern tube, pin and sew the units from Step 7 together as shown. Press the seams open as you sew, rotating the tube around the ironing board. Referring to Marking and Cutting the Pattern Tube on page 17, mark dots and connect with a drawn line as shown.

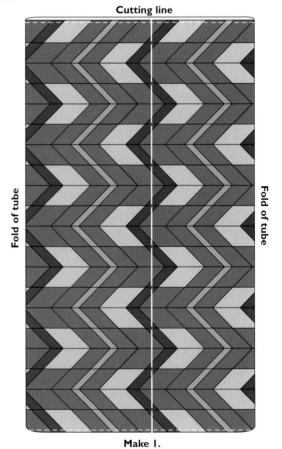

Make 1.

9. Using scissors, cut on the drawn line through one layer of the pattern tube to make it into a flat rectangle as shown. Mark dots and connect to make three cutting lines as shown. Using a rotary cutter and ruler, cut along the cutting lines to make 4 sub-units.

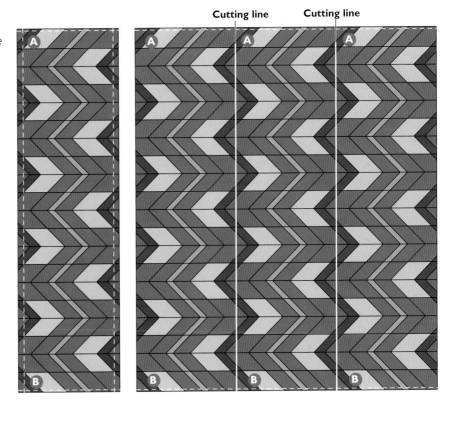

10. Pin 2 sub-units from Step 9 together along the marked seamline, matching the mirror-image pattern as shown. Sew, using a generous 1/2" seam allowance. Press the seams open. Make 2.

Make 2.

11. Pin both units from Step 10 together along the marked seamline to make one rectangle as shown. Sew, using a generous $1/2$" seam allowance, and press the seams open. Mark dots, making sure you mark them along the raw edges inward $1/4$" and $1/2$" as shown to allow for the seam allowances. Use a rotary cutter and ruler to cut along cutting line 1 to make 2 sub-units labeled C and D as shown.

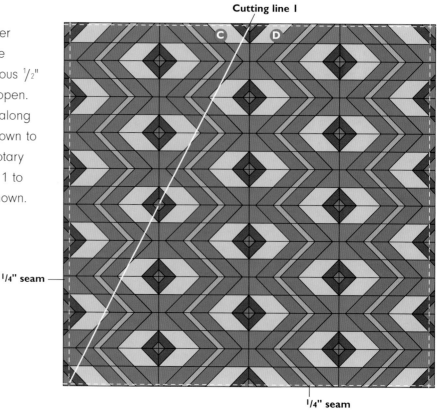

Cutting line 1

$1/4$" seam

$1/4$" seam

12. Rearrange sub-units C and D as shown. Matching the seams along the marked seamline, pin and sew these sub-units into a diamond, using a generous $1/2$" seam allowance. Press the seam open.

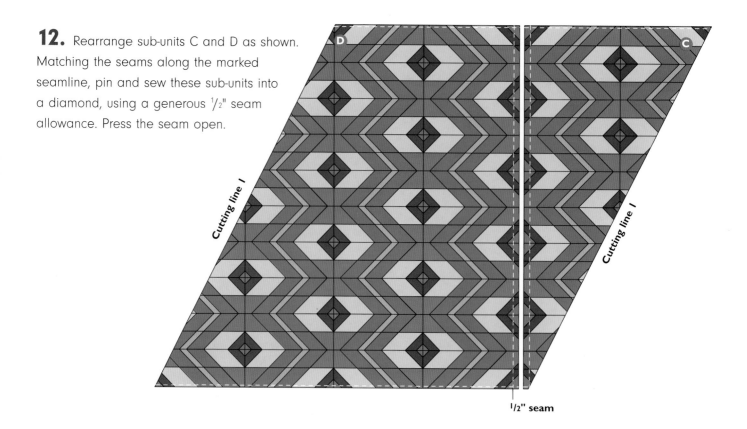

Cutting line 1

Cutting line 1

$1/2$" seam

13. Mark dots and draw cutting line 2 square to cutting line 1 as shown. Use a rotary cutter and ruler to cut on cutting line 2, making the diamond unit from Step 12 into 2 sub-units labeled "Top left of quilt" and "Bottom left of quilt."

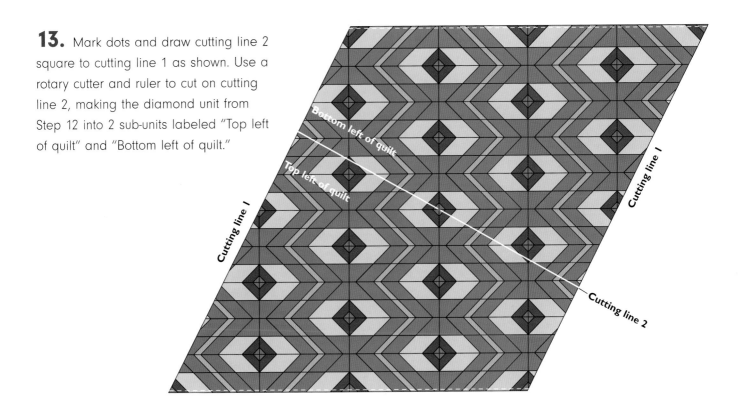

14. Rearrange the sub-units labeled "Top left of quilt" and "Bottom left of quilt." Match the mirror-image pattern along the marked seamline and pin. Using a 1/4" seam allowance, sew together as shown. Press the seam open.

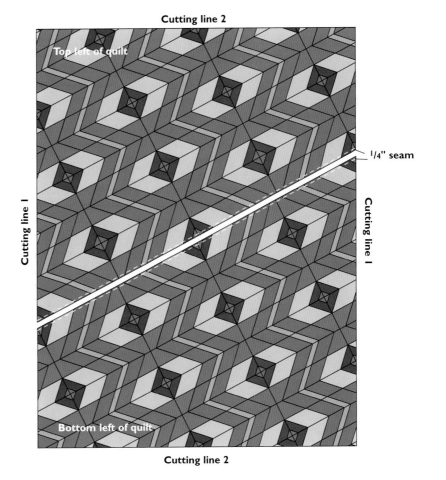

15. Refer to page 76 for tips and information
to help you complete your quilt.

Cutting line 2

Cutting line 1

Cutting line 1

Cutting line 2

Another Version - *Lightning Bolts.*
Designed, made, and quilted by Rita
Hutchens, 1986.
Finished size: 48" x 34".
This quilt is made of two mirror-image quilts
combined into one. I used the purple to tone
down the orange and fuchsia.

Designed and made by Rita Hutchens and quilted by Dawn Kelly, 2002. Finished size: 40" x 56"

In my rendition of the Irish Chain, I've used animal print fabrics with spots, but it's also an excellent design to make with solid colors. I've made many variations of this pattern and discovered that it is the most dramatic when made in fabrics that graduate in value.

Fabric Requirements and Cutting List

All yardages given are based on 42"-wide fabric, and strips are cut the full width of the fabric. Refer to Cutting the Strips on page 12.

FABRIC	AMOUNT	CUTTING
Six fabrics that graduate in value from light to dark	$^3/_4$ yard of each	Twelve strips 2" of each
Back	$2^5/_8$ yards	
Batting	46" x 62" piece	
Binding	$1^1/_3$ yards	six $6^1/_2$" strips

Working in Mirror Image

A completely new range of design options opens up when you work with symmetrical patterns. Any of these symmetrical patterns can be made into a mirror-image design without the use of templates. To make mirror-image designs using square patterns, the continuous strips are rotated in opposite directions for each mirror image. The tubes made at the beginning of Irish Chain Goes on Safari *are good examples. Make one mirror image following the diagrams, and make the other mirror image by repeating each step exactly the opposite way you did in the first mirror image.*

Directions

1. Referring to Sewing the Strips Together on page 13, sew the strips together as shown into 6 identical strip sets. Press the seams open as you sew. Referring to Squaring, Trimming, and Cutting on page 13, square and trim the ends of the strip sets. Cut each strip set in half crosswise. You will now have 12 strip sets, each approximately 21" in width.

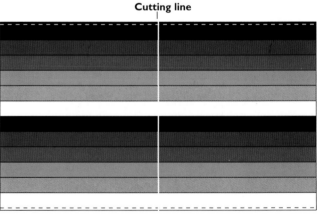

Cutting line

Make 6.

2. Sew the strip sets from Step 1 together as shown to make a strip band. Press the seams open as you sew. Make 6. Note the fold lines as shown.

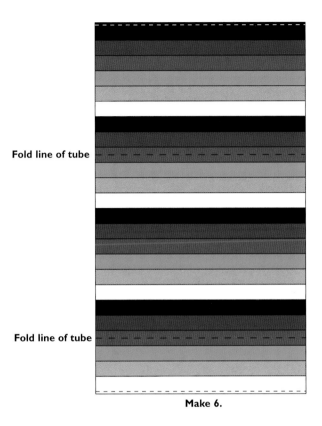

Fold line of tube

Fold line of tube

Make 6.

3. Sew the top of the strip band from Step 2 to the bottom of the same strip band, making a tube. Make 6 tubes. Press the seams open, placing the tube around the ironing board. Fold the tube on the fold line as shown. Check to make sure the seams are parallel to the fold of the tube. Referring to Cutting Continuous Strips on page 15, use a rotary cutter and ruler to cut through both layers of the tube to cut ten 2" continuous strips from the 6 tubes.

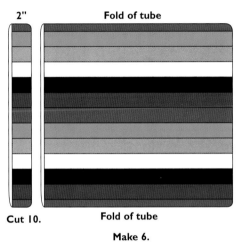

2"   **Fold of tube**

Cut 10.   **Fold of tube**

Make 6.

4. Line up pairs of continuous strips from Step 4 as shown. There will be 30 pairs.

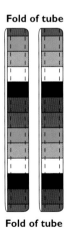

Fold of tube

Fold of tube

5A. This quilt is a mirror-image design in which you will be working with two patterns that are the reverse, or mirror image, of each other. To make mirror image A, rotate the right-hand continuous strip from Step 4 upward to make the pattern as shown. Pin together matching seams and sew. Press the seams open, rotating the continuous strips around the ironing board. Make 15 pairs.

Fold of tube

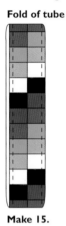

Make 15.

5B. To make mirror image B, rotate the right-hand continuous strip from Step 4 downward to make the pattern as shown. Pin together matching seams and sew. Press the seams open, rotating the continuous strips around the ironing board. Make 15 pairs.

Fold of tube

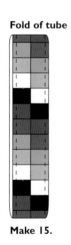

Make 15.

6A. To make the pattern tube for mirror image A, pin and sew 3 pairs of continuous strips from Step 5A together as shown. When you are matching up the pattern, always rotate the right-hand group of continuous strips upward as shown. Make 5 pattern tubes for mirror image A. Press the seams open as you sew. Referring to Marking and Cutting the Pattern Tube on page 17, mark dots, marking the first dot on the seam between the two middle values as shown. Make sure you mark the dots along the raw edge on the $1/4$" seam allowance. Rotate the tube as you mark the dots. Using your ruler, connect the dots with a drawn line. Rotate the tube as you draw the line as well.

Fold of tube

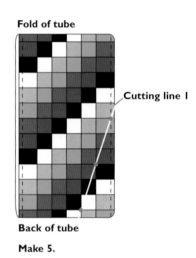

Cutting line I

Back of tube

Make 5.

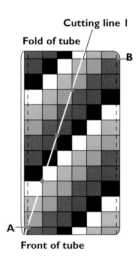

Cutting line I

Fold of tube

B

A

Front of tube

6B. To make and mark the pattern tube for mirror image B, repeat the steps in 6A, this time rotating the right-hand group downward as shown. (The lines will go in opposite directions.) Make 5 pattern tubes for mirror image B.

7. Using scissors, cut on the drawn line through one layer of each pattern tube to make it into a flat diamond shape. Mark the dots as shown. Mark dots near the raw edges on the $1/4$" seam allowance. Connect the dots with cutting lines 2 and 3 as shown. Repeat to make 5 for each mirror image.

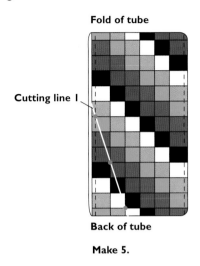

Fold of tube

Cutting line 1

Back of tube

Make 5.

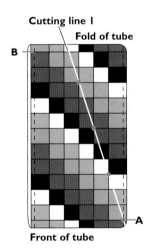

Cutting line 1

Fold of tube

B

A

Front of tube

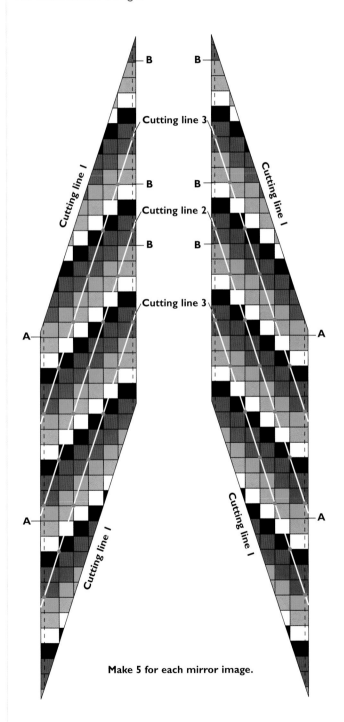

Make 5 for each mirror image.

IRISH CHAIN GOES ON SAFARI **55**

8. Using a rotary cutter and ruler, cut the diamond shapes from Step 7 on cutting line 2 to make two equal units. Arrange these units, matching seam A to seam B, the cutting line, and all other matching seams as shown. Repeat for the 5 units of each mirror image.

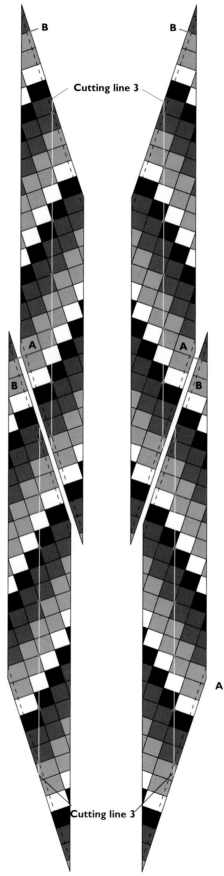

Make 5 for each mirror image.

9. Continue to work in mirror images, keeping the pieces of each mirror image separate from the pieces of the other. Pin and sew the units from Step 8 together along the marked seamline, matching the cutting lines of the two pieces, seam A of one piece to seam B of the other, and all other matching seams as shown. Press the seams open as you sew. Repeat for the 5 units of each mirror image.

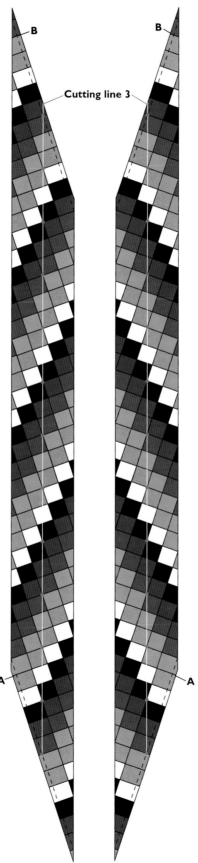

Make 5 for each mirror image.

10. To make another tube, bring the seam at point A up to match the seam at point B and pin. Pin the other matching seams along this edge and sew, easing in flatness. The seam will spiral around the tube. Place the tube around the ironing board, and press the seam open. The flat diamond shape becomes a tube again. Make 5 for each mirror image.

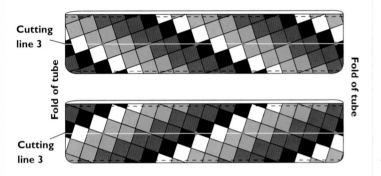

11. Using scissors, cut through one layer of the tube along cutting line 3 shown in Step 10, making 2 continuous strips from the tube. Repeat for all 5 tubes of each mirror image, making 10 continuous strips for each mirror image.

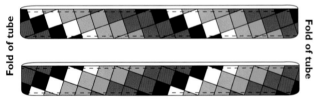

Make 10 for each mirror image.

12. Sew one mirror image unit from Step 11 together with an opposite mirror image unit, matching the mirror-image pattern. Make sure the light and dark values match up as shown. Press the seams open, rotating the tube around the ironing board. Mark dots on the $^1/_4$" seamline as shown. Make 10.

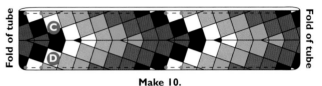

Make 10.

13. Line up units from Step 12 as shown. (You will be joining seams from the same mirror image.) Pin, matching dots, and sew. Press the seams open, rotating the tube around the ironing board. Make 4. There will be 2 units leftover. Set one aside to use in Step 15. Use the remaining leftover unit as the start of a pillow to match your quilt or for the beginning of another quilt.

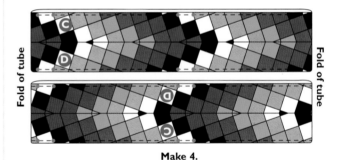

Make 4.

14. Pin and sew the units from Step 13 together, matching dots as shown. As in Step 13, you are joining seams from the same mirror image.

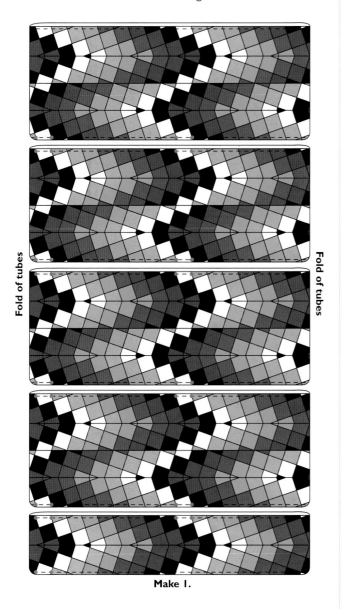

Make 1.

15. Sew all the units together, including one of the leftover units from Step 13, to complete the pattern tube as shown. Mark dots and cutting line 4 square to the ends and parallel to the fold of the tube as shown.

16. Using scissors, cut through one layer of the tube to make the quilt.

17. Refer to page 76 for tips and information to help you complete your quilt.

Top left of quilt **Cutting line 4**

Bottom left of quilt **Cutting line 4**

Another Version - *Irish Chain on the Homestead*.

Designed and made by Rita Hutchens and quilted

by Dawn Kelly, 2002.

Finished size: 30" x 30".

This variation was made using the same continuous

strips, this time rotated and cut kaleidoscope fashion.

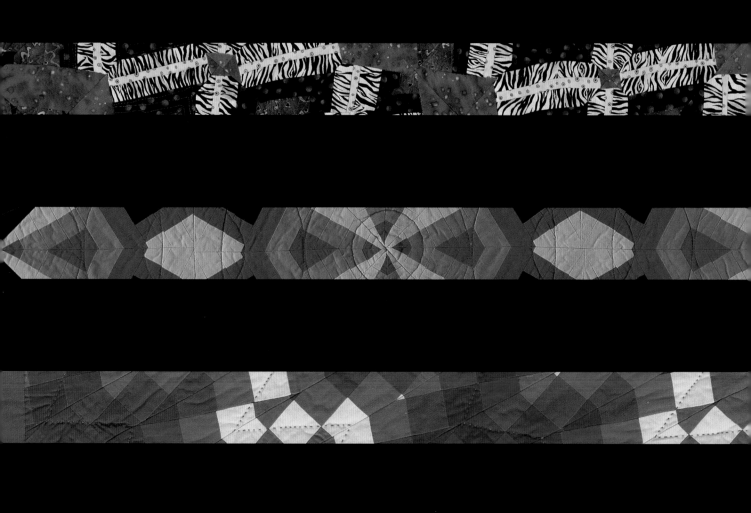

GALLERY OF QUILTS

I am fascinated with figuring out how to make different patterns and exploring their possible variations. One pattern leads to another, one color combination leads to another, and one quilt leads to another—a continuous process of creating and discovering. I have dreamed up many different concepts for making quilts over the years, and the following quilts show some of the results.

After my initial discovery of quiltmaking, I made quilts with only solid colors, and continued to do so for twelve years. It was a great exercise, enabling me to develop patterns without the added confusion of printed fabric. The first four quilts were made during this time. It is only in the last nine years that I have been using printed fabric.

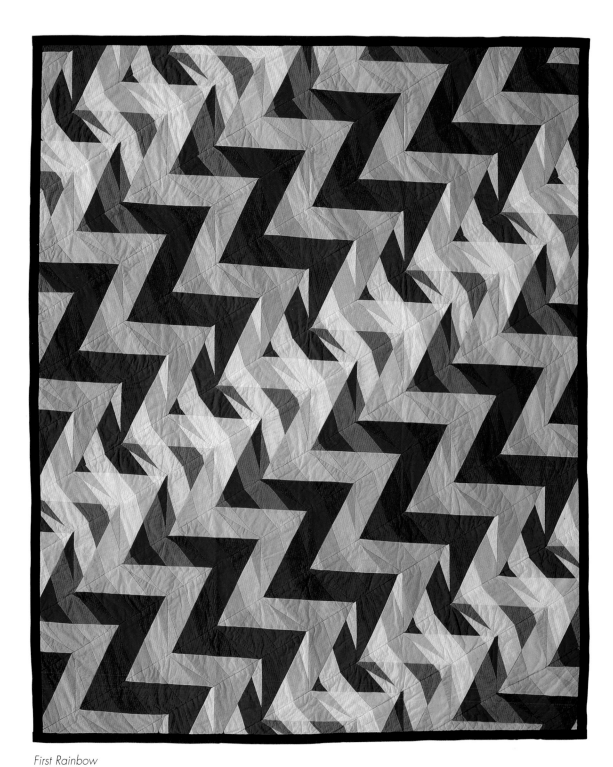

First Rainbow

Designed, made, and quilted

by Rita Hutchens, 1986.

Finished size: 62" x 76"

I did a whole series of quilts in mirror image,

exploring the use of light and dark values of the

same colors. This is my favorite quilt of the series.

Choice Seconds

Designed, made, and quilted

by Rita Hutchens, 1986.

Finished size: 52" x 54"

Another quilt from the same series

exploring value made in secondary colors.

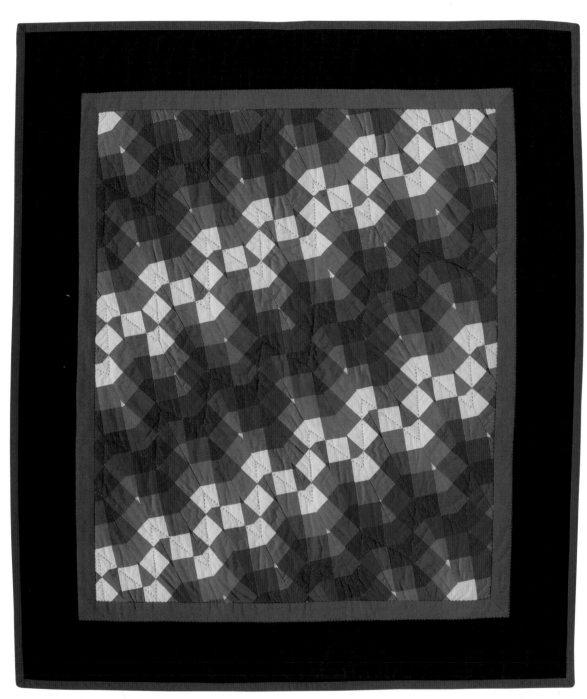

Another Rainbow
Designed, made, and quilted
by Rita Hutchens, 1987.
Finished size: 34" x 39"
This quilt is a variation of the *Irish Chain* project on page 50—a good pattern to use with solid colors.

Wagon Wheels
Designed, made, and quilted
by Rita Hutchens, 1994.
Finished size: 36" x 36"
This was the first quilt I made using a
90° mirror-image design. I used the same
technique, which can be done with any mirror-image pattern, to create *Irish Chain on
the Homestead* on page 61.

Through a forced change in lifestyle, I gave up quilting for a while. When I picked it up again, I did not want to do the same stuff I had been doing. I decided it was time to take some classes to get out and see what other quilters were doing, to become inspired, and to learn new techniques I could apply to my own work. I was inspired, and did pick up some new techniques which I immediately transferred to my own work. I designed and made the following quilts after I began taking classes.

Chris's Quilt
Designed, made, quilted, and embellished with beads
by Rita Hutchens, 1998.
Finished size: 48" x 48"
I had done mirror-image patterns before, but this was the first time
I began to think of my mirror-image patterns as kaleidoscopes.
This was one of the first quilts I made with printed fabrics.

Clowning Around

Designed, made, quilted, and embellished with beads
by Rita Hutchens, 1998.

Finished size: 32" x 32"

I was just clowning around when I made this quilt in
which I started using chartreuse green and stripes.
I used to force myself not to use purple. Lately I
challenge myself not to use chartreuse green.

Ornament
Designed and made by
Rita Hutchens and quilted
by Dawn Kelly, 2001.
Finished size: 30" x 30"
Here is another good example of a 90°
mirror-image design. I am not too concerned
with perfectly matching seams. I think being
"consistently inconsistent" adds a lot of character to my work.

Celtic Knot
Designed, made, and quilted
by Rita Hutchens, 2000.
Finished size: 35" x 35"
This quilt was made completely without rulers, using
continuous strip piecing. I made it after taking a class
on curved strip piecing that opened up a whole new
way of working. It was a great revelation.

Tumbling Dice
Designed, made, and quilted
by Rita Hutchens, 2002.
Finished size: 34" x 34"
A little color goes a long way when you are
working with black and white—particularly
stripes—to create a quilt with a bold look.

Dancing Hearts
Designed, made, and quilted
by Rita Hutchens, 2002.
Finished size: 18" x 18"
I made this variation of *Tumbling Dice*
(page 72) using hearts instead of cross
shapes. Even the hearts were made using
continuous strip piecing.

Lucky Sixes
Designed, made, and quilted
by Rita Hutchens, 2002.
Finished size: 21" x 22"
I cut the leftovers from *Tumbling Dice*
(page 72) into wedges to make this quilt.

Blooming Flowers

Designed and made by

Rita Hutchens and quilted by Roberta Rose-Kanauth, 2002.

Finished size: 50" x 56"

This quilt started with hearts, which I was not happy with. Luckily, the other fabrics in the quilt landed next to them on my studio floor and inspired me. I stopped what I was doing and this quilt poured out of me. You know you're on the right track when that happens.

General Instructions

There are as many different ways of finishing a quilt as there are quilters. Finishing is just as important as any other element in the quilt. If you are planning to enter your quilt in a show, the finishing work is what might get your quilt into the show over that of another. I will tell you what works for me, and I've included a list of books in Resources on page 79 that explain these and other finishing techniques in detail if you need more direction.

Squaring the Quilt

Be sure that your quilt is completely square whether or not you plan to add borders. Spray the quilt with a spray bottle, and use a hot steam iron to iron the quilt as flat as possible to block it. Fold the quilt in half, right side out. Use two rulers to trim it as little as possible to make it square. Place one ruler on the fold of the quilt and the other ruler on the raw edges of the folded quilt perpendicular to the first as shown. Using your rotary cutter along the ruler on the raw edges, trim through both layers of the folded quilt. Check to see if your quilt is square by folding it in the other direction and comparing the lengths of the two edges that are parallel to the fold. Trim to make any necessary adjustments.

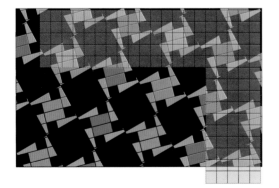

Borders

The border is the last thing added to the quilt top, and should appear as part of the quilt—not as an afterthought. I think borders are appropriate on some, but not all, quilts. This is an aesthetic decision, based on composition and reserved for the maker of the quilt.

When the quilt does call for a border, I prefer a mitered border, which makes a crisp, clean corner. I often use stripes, symmetrical fabrics, or pieced patterns made using my technique in my borders, all of which frame the quilt nicely. Sometimes several wide and narrow borders are called for in the same quilt. You can be really creative and use a different border on every side of your quilt. Sometimes I prefer a wide binding instead of the border. I invite you to be as creative with your borders as you are with the rest of your quilt.

Layering and Basting

Cut the backing and batting at least 6" longer and wider than the quilt top. Layer the backing, batting, and quilt top, leaving at least 3" of batting and backing extending on all sides. Smooth out any folds.
If you are machine quilting, baste the quilt together using curved quilters' safety pins. This is much faster than thread basting, and when you remove the pins as you quilt, the quilted texture becomes more visible. I also prefer using pins for basting when I am hand quilting.

Quilting

The quilting should enhance the quilt by adding line, texture, and relief to accentuate the pattern, fabric, color, and values. Quilting is as important as every other aspect of your quilt, so take the time to decide what should be done.

Study the quilt to determine what moves forward visually and what recedes. Darker values will tend to recede and lighter values will tend to move forward. More quilting in areas that recede more than areas that move forward, adds texture to complement what is already there. Use contrasting threads to add more relief, or matching threads to add less relief to your quilt. Look for some element of repetition in the pattern or fabrics of the quilt and carry that over to the quilting. Think about the effects a straight line will have on your pattern as opposed to a curved line.

For possible quilting ideas, make a copy of a photo of your quilt and doodle on it for inspiration, or put a large piece of clear vinyl over the actual quilt and draw quilting lines with an erasable marker. If you are taking your quilt to a professional quilter, be specific about what you want. You will see details in your quilts no one else will see.

Sleeve for Hanging

Adding a sleeve to the back of your quilt is a good way to ensure that someone won't put tacks or nails into your quilt in an attempt to hang it. A sleeve is essential if you plan to enter your quilt in any show. I suggest making a sleeve that is at least 4"-wide as this is what most shows require.

Binding

I use a double-fold binding with a mitered corner. I cut the strips for the binding on the grain unless there is a pattern in the fabric—such as a stripe—that I want to cut on the bias, or if the quilt has a curved edge. I determine the width of the binding according to what works best visually for the quilt. I tend to put wider bindings on quilts that do not have a border and use narrower bindings when I want to accent a zinger color in the quilt. I sew the binding to the quilt with a seam equal in width to the width of finished binding.

Labels

If you were a painter, you wouldn't think about not signing a painting. Just as for a painting, signing and dating your quilts gives them value. There are many different ways to sign your quilts, such as with hand or machine embroidery or textile markers. I like to make a label by using some of the leftover pieces from the quilt itself,

or by designing a label on my computer. I then print it on an iron-on transfer, iron it to a piece of white fabric, and sew it to the quilt. There are lots of other good products for printing on fabric from your computer, such as *Bubble Jet Set*. Create your own style for your labels and use it on all of your quilts.

Embellishing

Embellishing is jewelry for a quilt. It adds sparkle and character along with another layer of relief and dimension, making your quilts even more individual, much like accessorizing a nice garment. There are many different ways to embellish a quilt, depending on your skills and what kind of jewelry you like.

You can embellish your quilt with thread work before you layer the quilt with batting and backing. There are many different threads available today in different finishes and many creative things you can do with them using your sewing machine. If you like hand embroidery, use this technique to add detail to your quilt as well.

You can also think of the actual quilting as an embellishment, and use threads that contrast with your fabric or a decorative hand or machine quilting stitch. Buttons, beads, or pins might be a unique way to hold the layers of your quilt together.

I am also a bead artist and, I collect beads just as I collect fabric. I have many different shapes, colors, finishes, and sizes, so putting them on my quilts seems a natural progression. Put beads on your quilt after you have completed any machine sewing or quilting. I like to put beads around the edges of my quilts like little Christmas lights. Sparkly beads float on dark fabric, adding dimension. I often emphasize the print of the fabric with beads.

Be careful. . . .once you start embellishing your quilts, they will seem incomplete until they are embellished!

About the Author

Rita lives in the small town of Sandpoint in the mountains of northern Idaho. Her workspace takes up half the living room of the home she shares with her teenage daughter, Aleya, who is also very creative.

Primarily self-taught with a strong determination to be unique, Rita's focus in quilting for the last 23 years has been to develop and refine her own style and way of working to create dramatically graphic quilts. In her first book, *Totally Tubular Quilts*, she shares this exciting and innovative technique with quilters.

In addition to quilting, Rita has used her passion for color and pattern to develop a unique style and technique of beading, which she uses to make one-of-a-kind and limited edition jewelry. She makes her living as a professional artist, creating and selling her work in beading and quilting, as well as teaching and writing about her inventive techniques in both disciplines.

With quilting and beading being such sedentary occupations, Rita likes to stay in shape being active in telemark skiing, biking, kayaking, gardening, and enjoying the outdoors in the beautiful area in which she lives.

Resources

Porcella, Yvonne. *Six Color World*. Lafayette, CA: C&T Publishing, 1997.

Torrence, Lorraine. *Design Essentials: The Quilters Guide*. Woodinville, WA: Martingale & Company, 1998.

Dudley, Taimi. *Strip Patchwork*. New York, NY: Van Nostrand Rienhold, 1980.

Bradkin, Cheryl Greider. *Basic Seminole Patterns*. Lafayette, CA: C&T Publishing, 1996.

Brackman, Barbara. *Encyclopedia of Pieced Quilt Patterns*. Paducah, KY: American Quilters Society, 1993.

All About Quilting. Lafayette, CA: C&T Publishing, 2002.

Collins, Sally. *Small Scale Quiltmaking*. Lafayette, CA: C&T Publishing, 1996.

Krentz, Jan. *Lone Star Quilts and Beyond*. Lafayette, CA: C&T Publishing, 2001.

Roberts, Sharee Dawn. *Creative Machine Art*. Paducah, KY: Collector Books, 1992.

Noble, Maureen. *Machine Quilting Made Easy*. Woodinville, WA: Martingale & Company, 1994.

Sassman, Jane. *The Quilted Garden*. Lafayette, CA: C&T Publishing, 2000.

Quilts from Europe: Projects and Inspirations. Lafayette, CA: C&T Publishing, 2000.

Shaw, Robert. *The Art Quilt*. Westport, CN: Hugh Lauter Levin Associates, Inc., 1997.

Other fine books from C&T Publishing

24 Quilted Gems: Sparkling Traditional & Original Projects, Gai Perry

250 More Continuous-Line Quilting Designs for Hand, Machine & Long-Arm Quilters, Laura Lee Fritz

All About Quilting from A to Z, From the Editors and Contributors of *Quilter's Newsletter Magazine* and *Quiltmaker* magazine

America from the Heart: Quilters Remember September 11, 2001, Karey Bresenhan

At Piece With Time: A Woman's Journey Stitched in Cloth, Kristin Steiner & Diane Frankenberger

Block Magic, Too!: Over 50 NEW Blocks from Squares and Rectangles, Nancy Johnson-Srebro

Celebrate the Tradition with C&T Publishing: Over 70 Fabulous New Blocks, Tips & Stories from Quilting's Best, C&T Staff

Fantastic Fans: Exquisite Quilts & Other Projects, Alice Dunsdon

Fast, Fun & Easy Fabric Bowls: 5 Reversible Shapes to Use & Display, Linda Johanson

Floral Affair, A: Quilts & Accessories for Romantics, Nihon Vogue

Flowering Favorites from Piece O' Cake Designs: Becky Goldsmith & Linda Jenkins

Hunter Star Quilts & Beyond: Jan Krentz

Liberated String Quilts, Gwen Marston

Make it Simpler Paper Piecing: Easy as 1-2-3 — A Pinless Fold & Sew Technique, Anita Grossman Solomon

New Look at Log Cabin Quilts, A: Design a Scene Block by Block PLUS 10 Easy-to-Follow Projects, Flavin Glover

Plentiful Possibilities: A Timeless Treasury of 16 Terrific Quilts, Lynda Milligan & Nancy Smith

Quick-Strip Paper Piecing: For Blocks, Borders & Quilts, Peggy Martin

Ricky Tims' Convergence Quilts: Mysterious, Magical, Easy, and Fun, Ricky Tims

Strips 'n Curves: A New Spin on Strip Piecing, Louisa L. Smith

Sweet Dreams, Moon Baby: A Quilt to Make, A Story to Read, Elly Sienkiewicz

Teddy Bear Redwork: • *25 Fresh, New Designs* • *Step-by-Step Projects* • *Quilts and More*, Jan Rapacz

When Quilters Gather: 20 Patterns of Piecers at Play, Ruth B. McDowell

For more information, ask for a free catalog:

C&T Publishing, Inc.
P.O. Box 1456
Lafayette, CA 94549
(800) 284-1114
Email: ctinfo@ctpub.com
Website: www.ctpub.com

For quilting supplies:

Cotton Patch Mail Order
3405 Hall Lane, Dept. CTB
Lafayette, CA 94549
(800) 835-4418
(925) 283-7883
Email:quiltusa@yahoo.com
Website: www.quiltusa.com

Note: Fabrics used in the quilts shown may not be currently available since fabric manufacturers keep most fabrics in print for only a short time.

Index